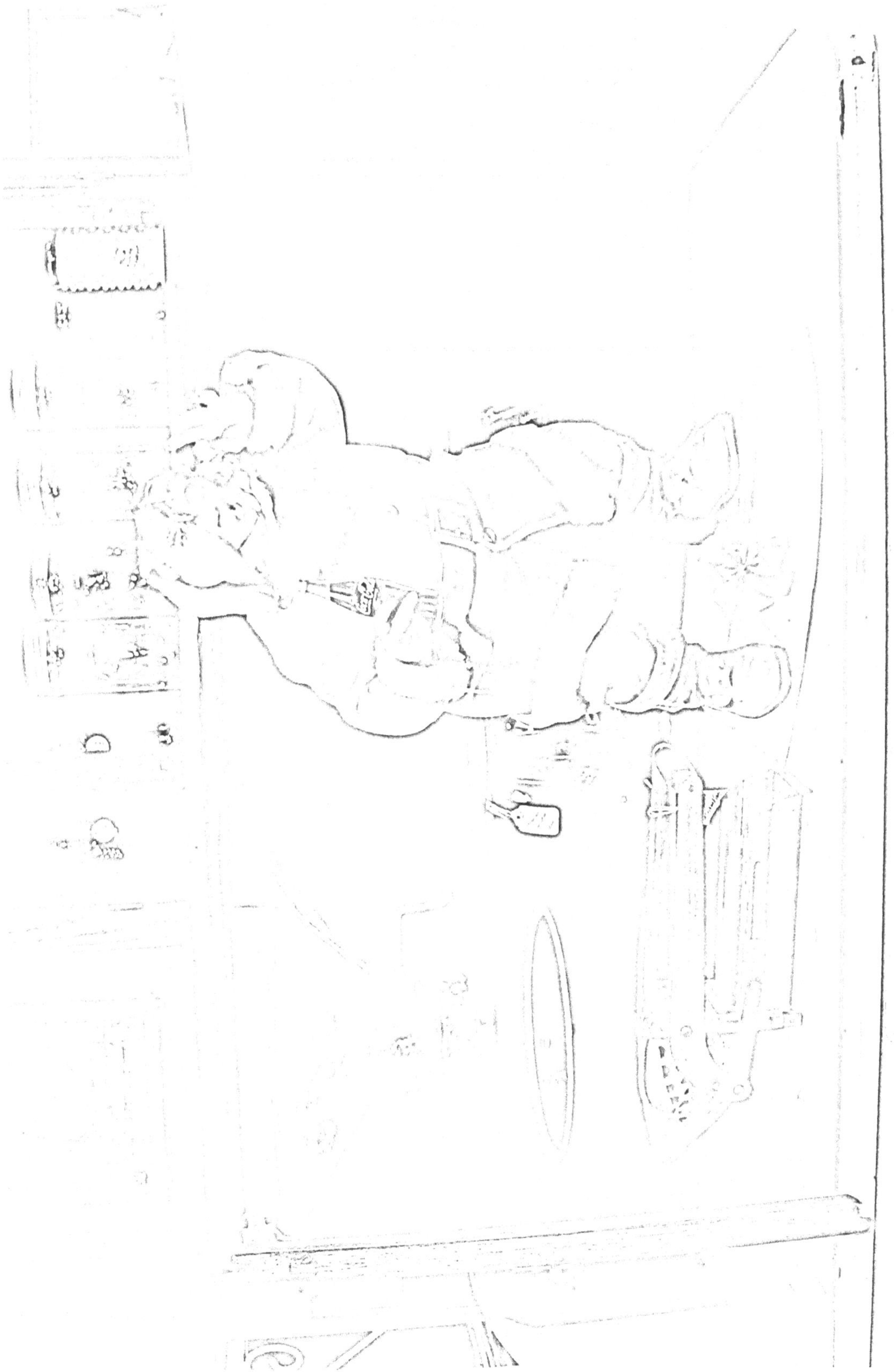

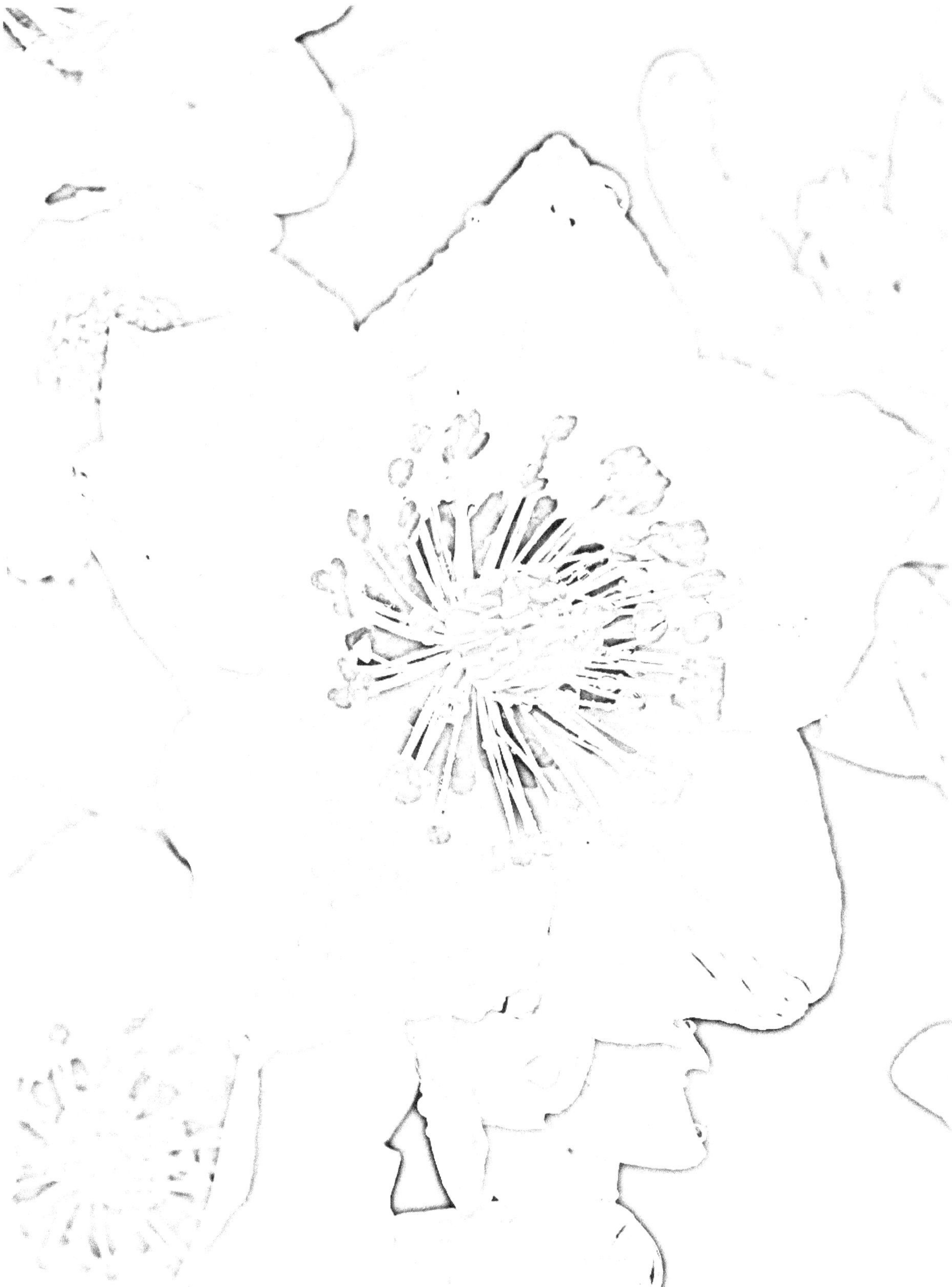

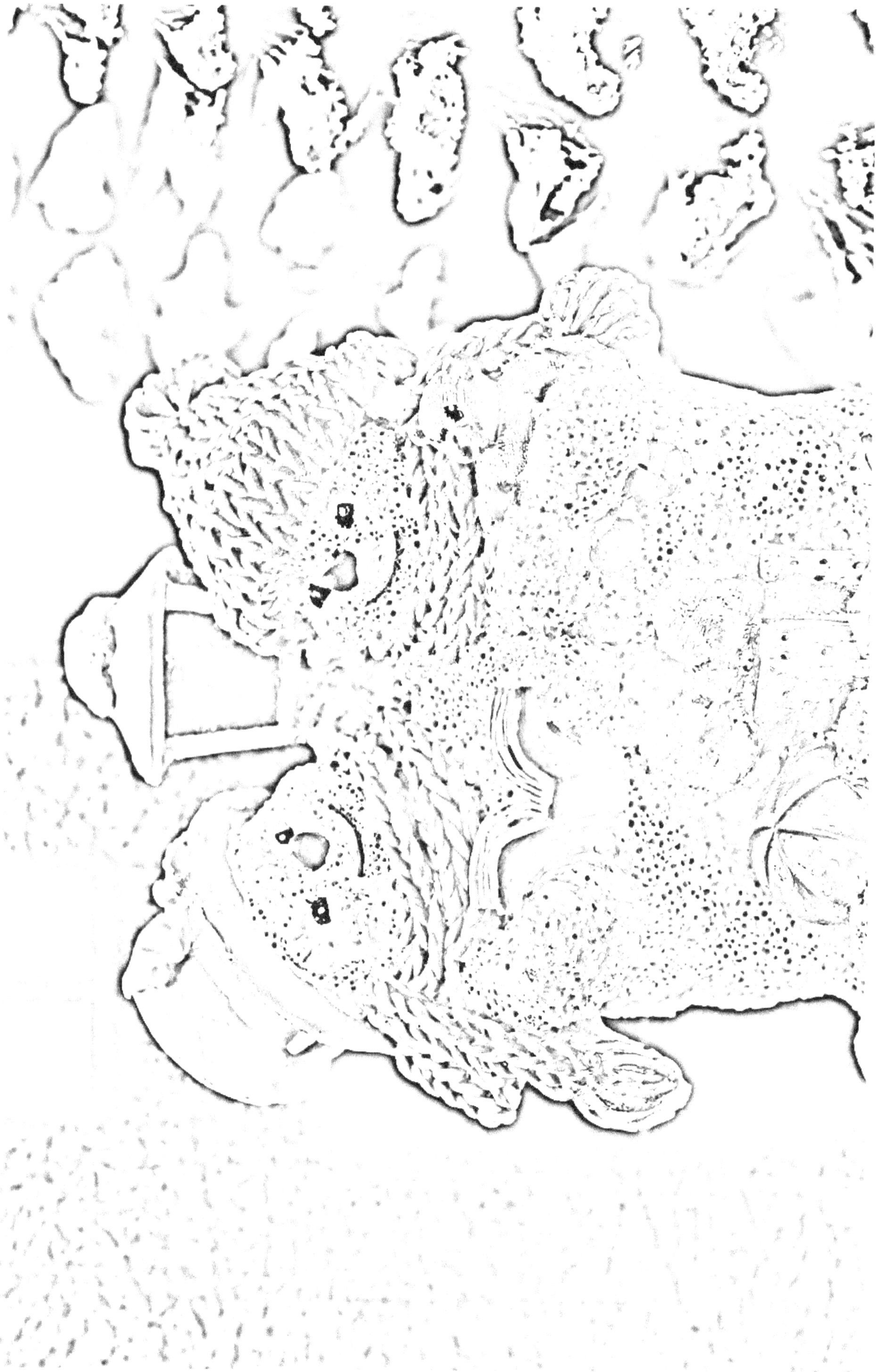

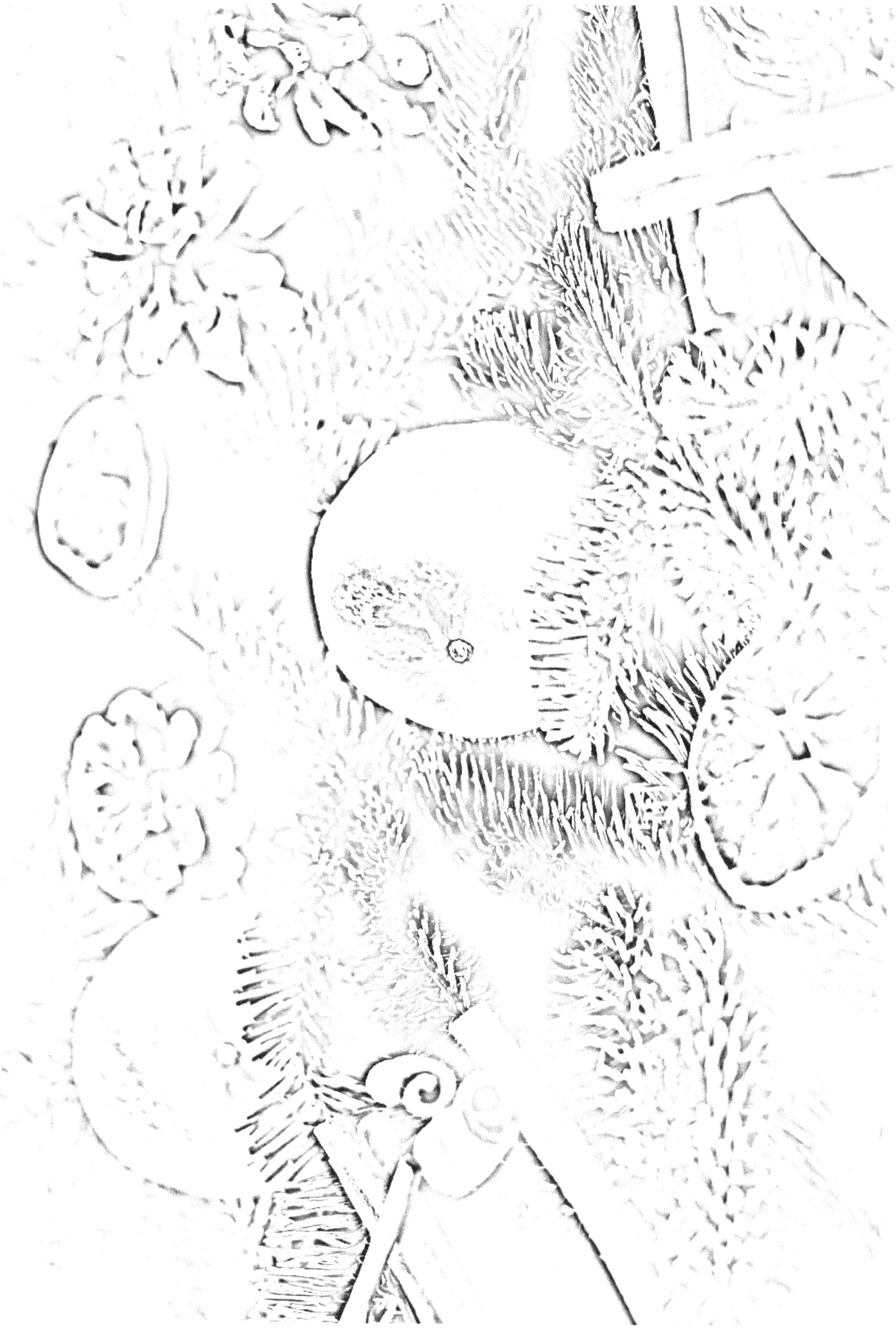

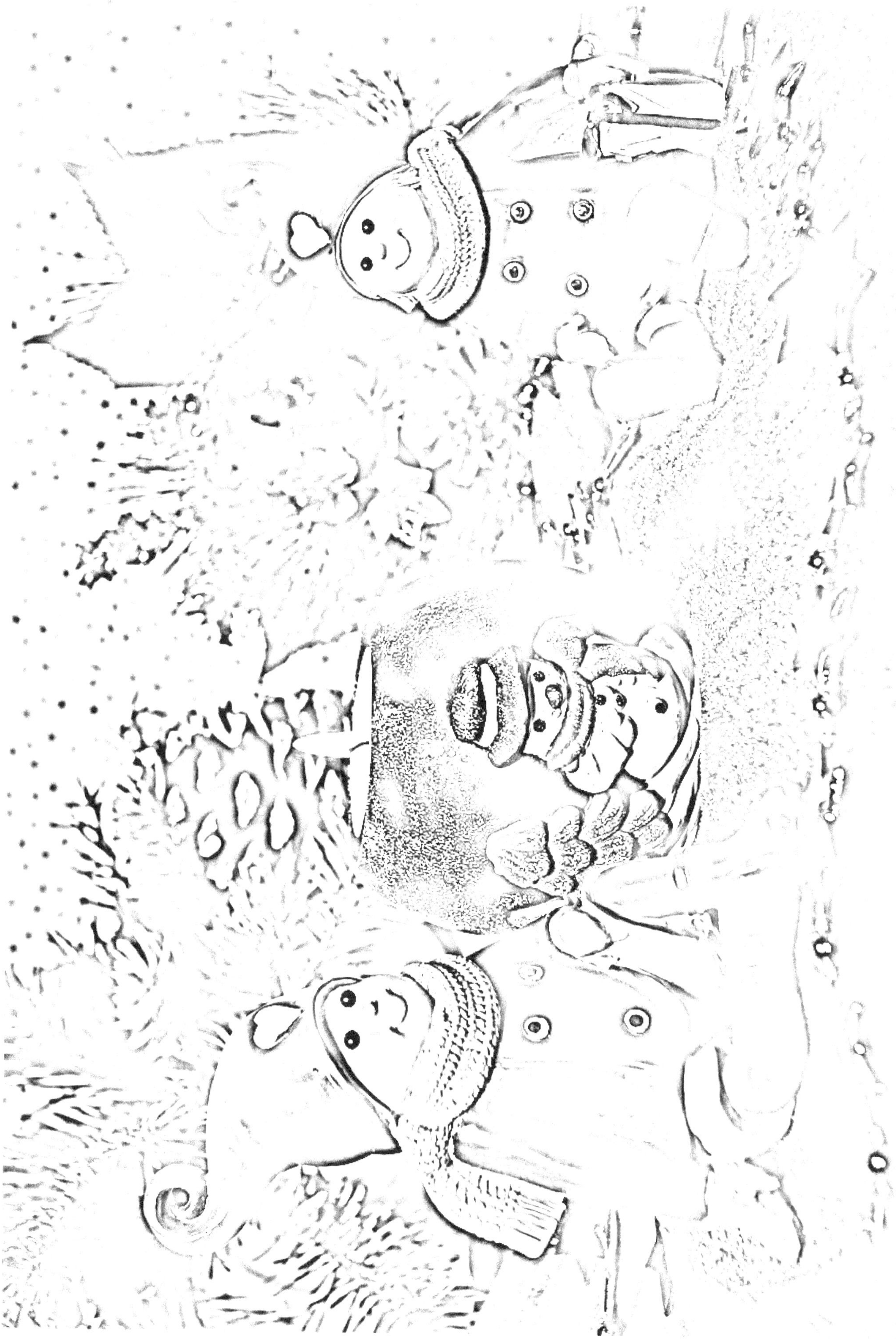

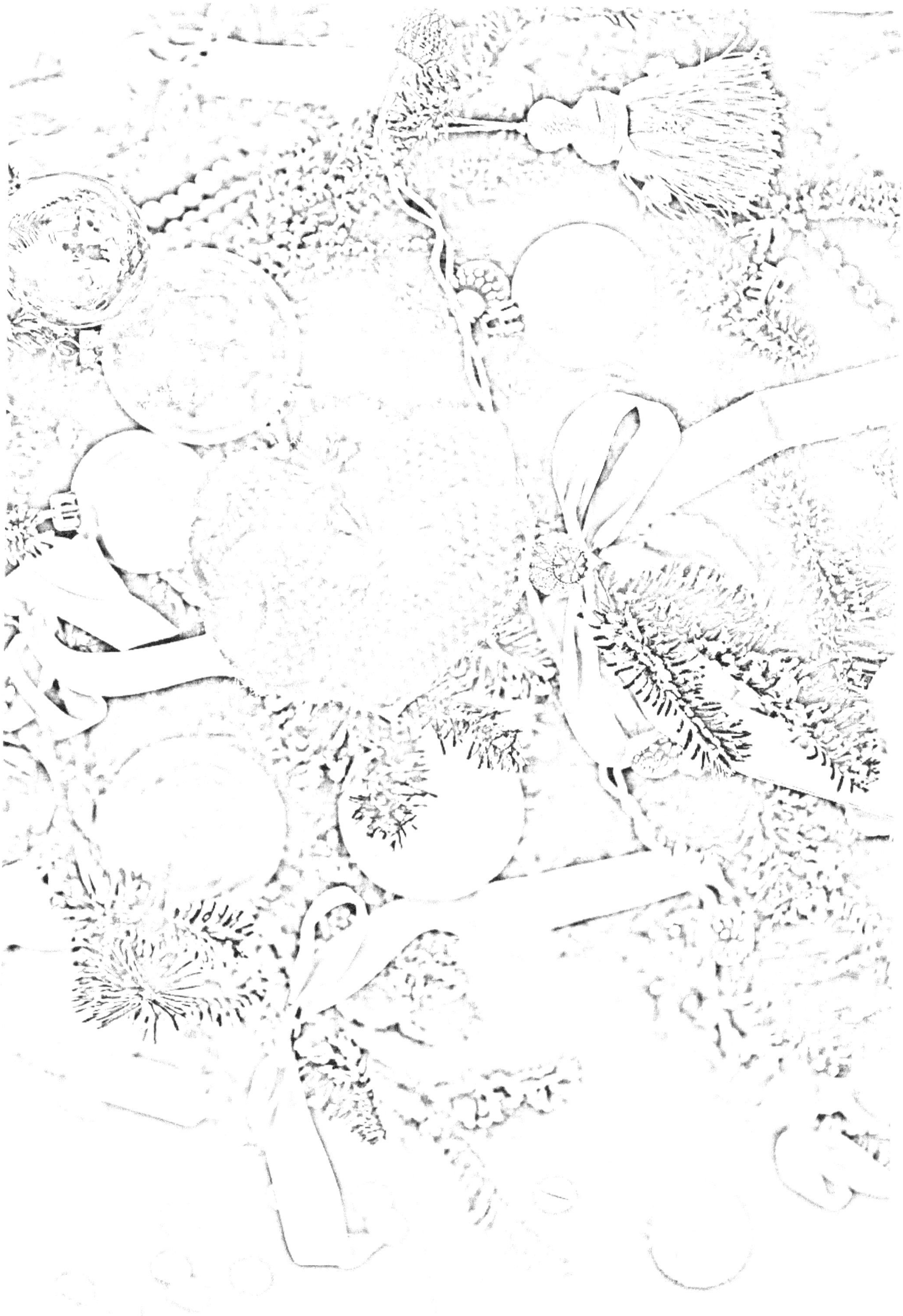

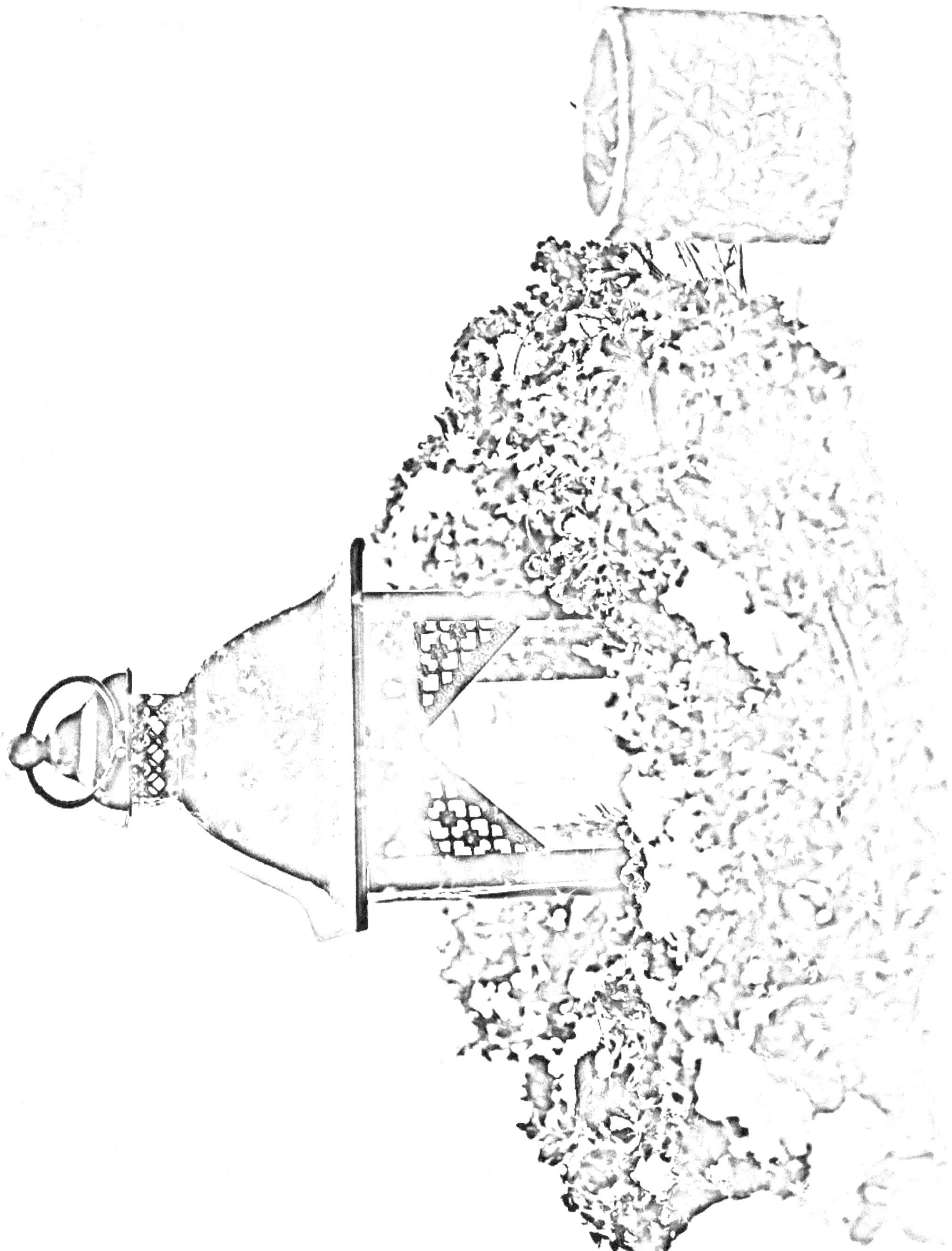

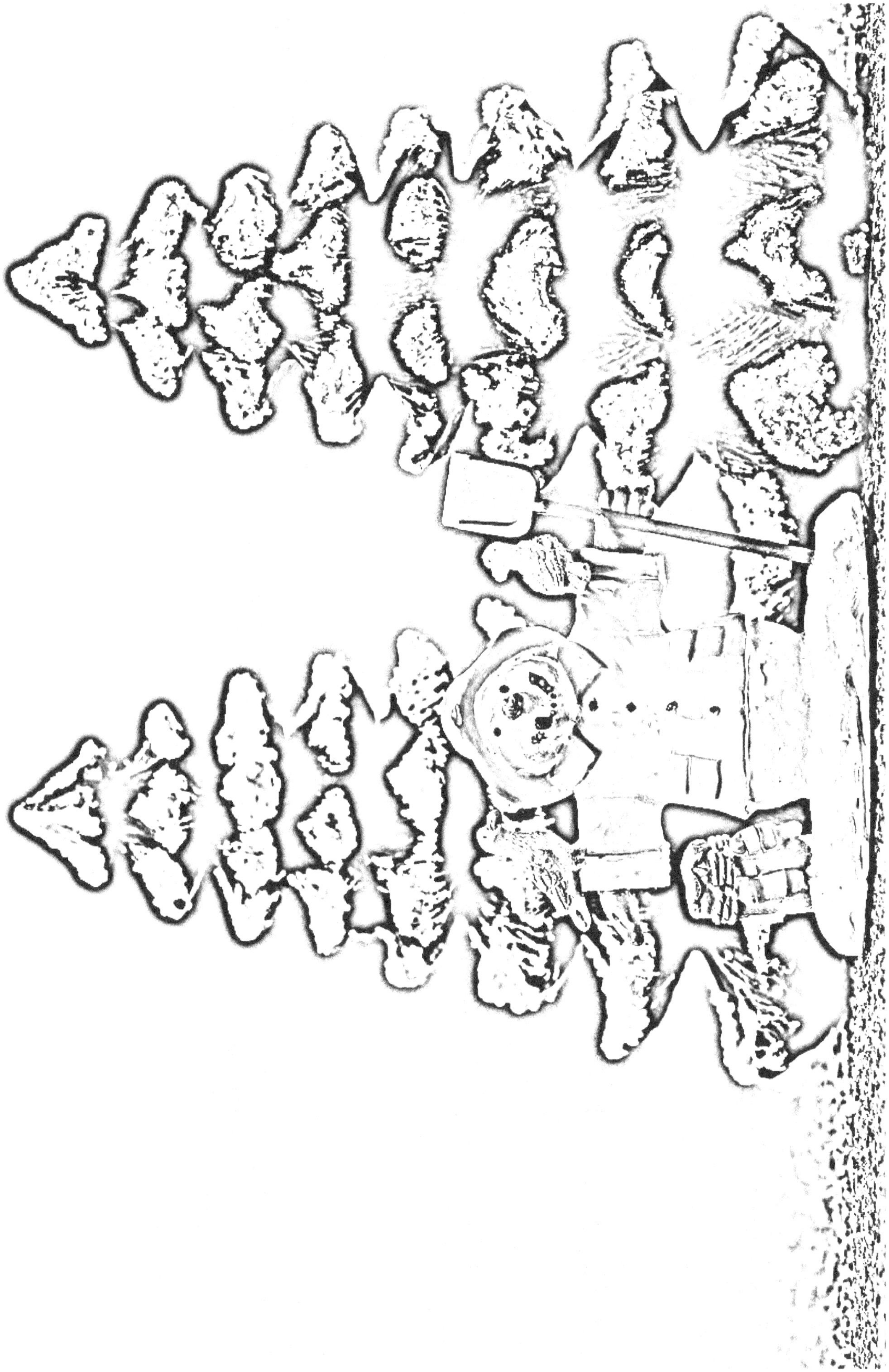

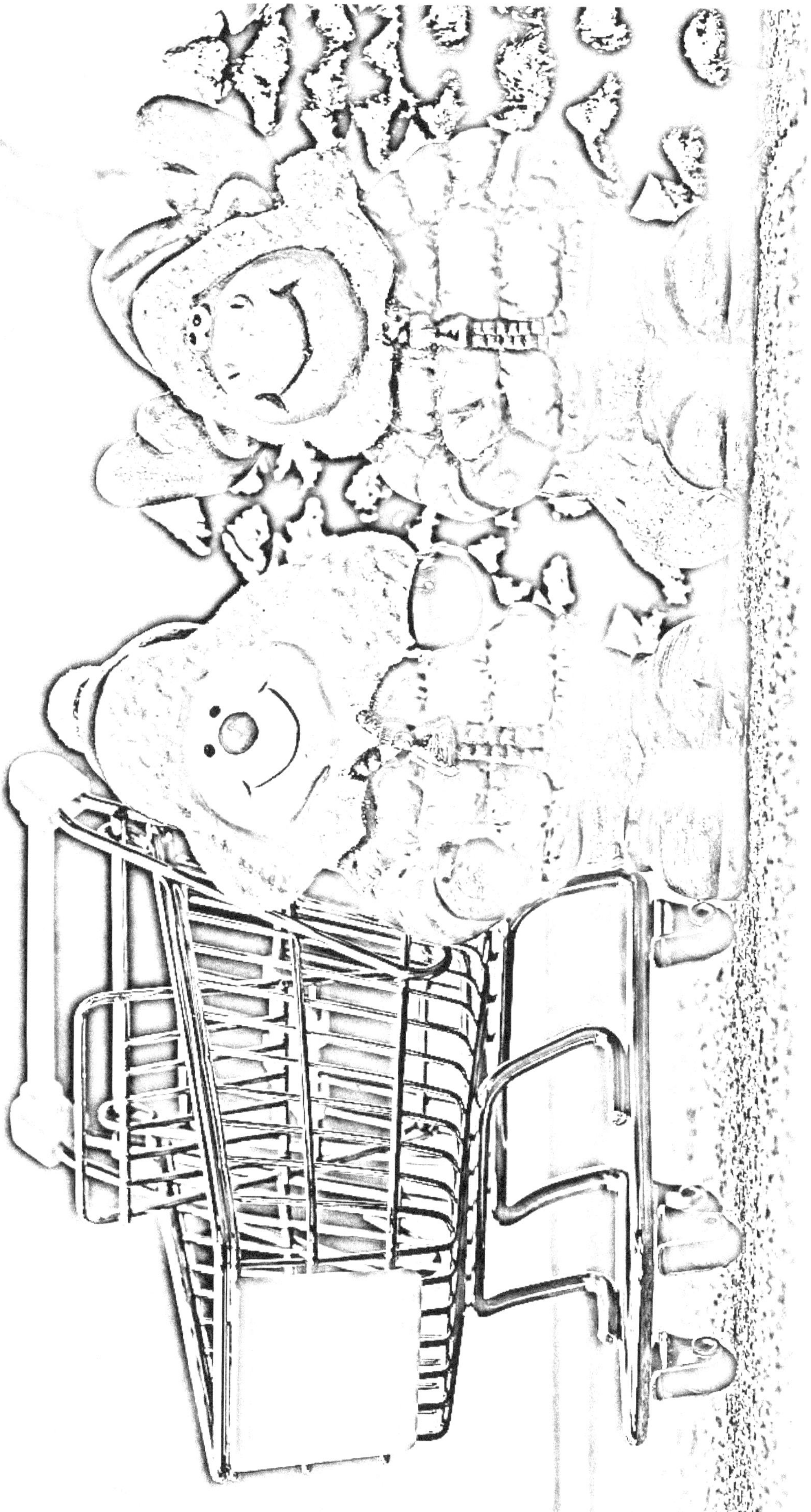

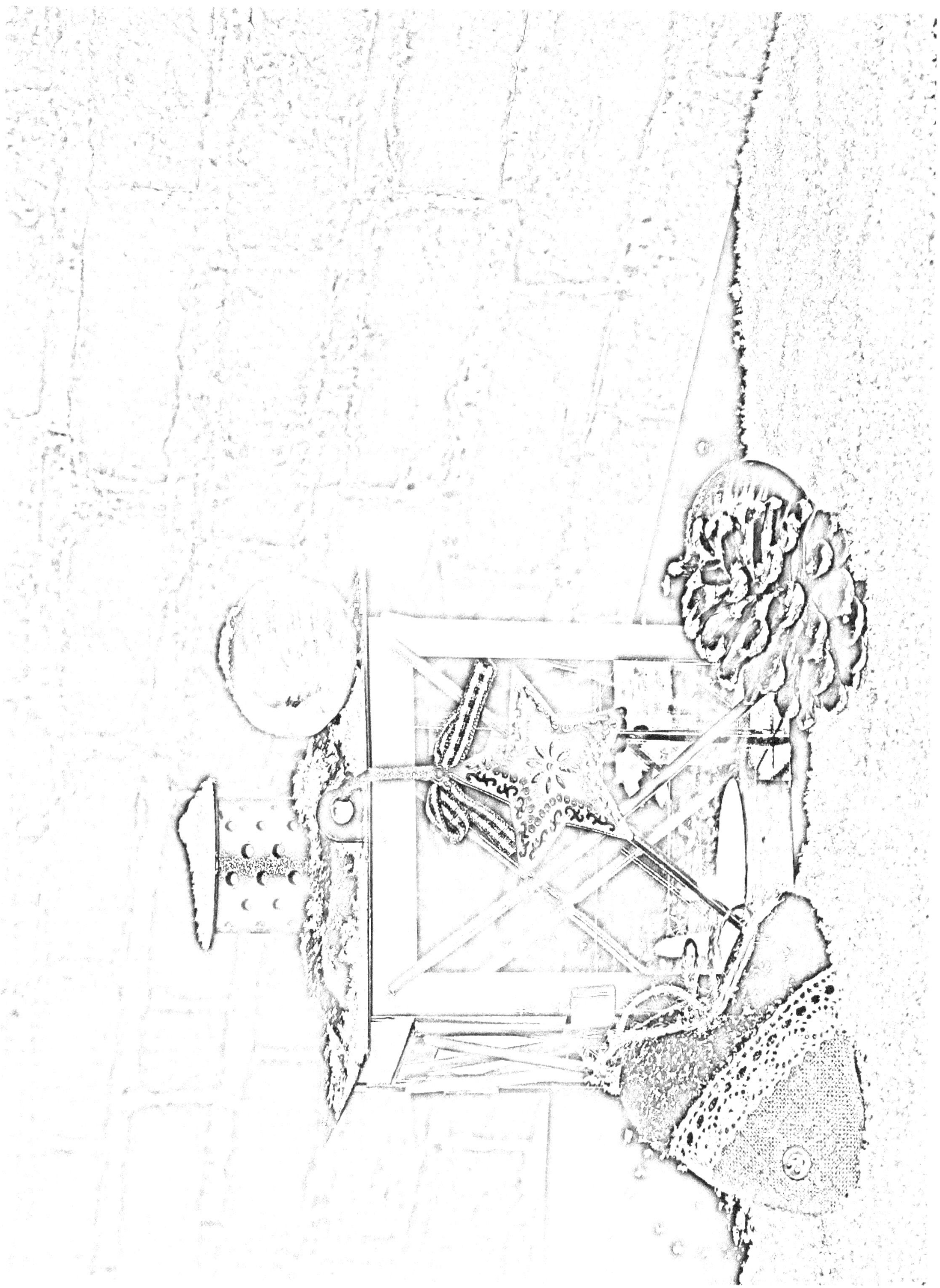

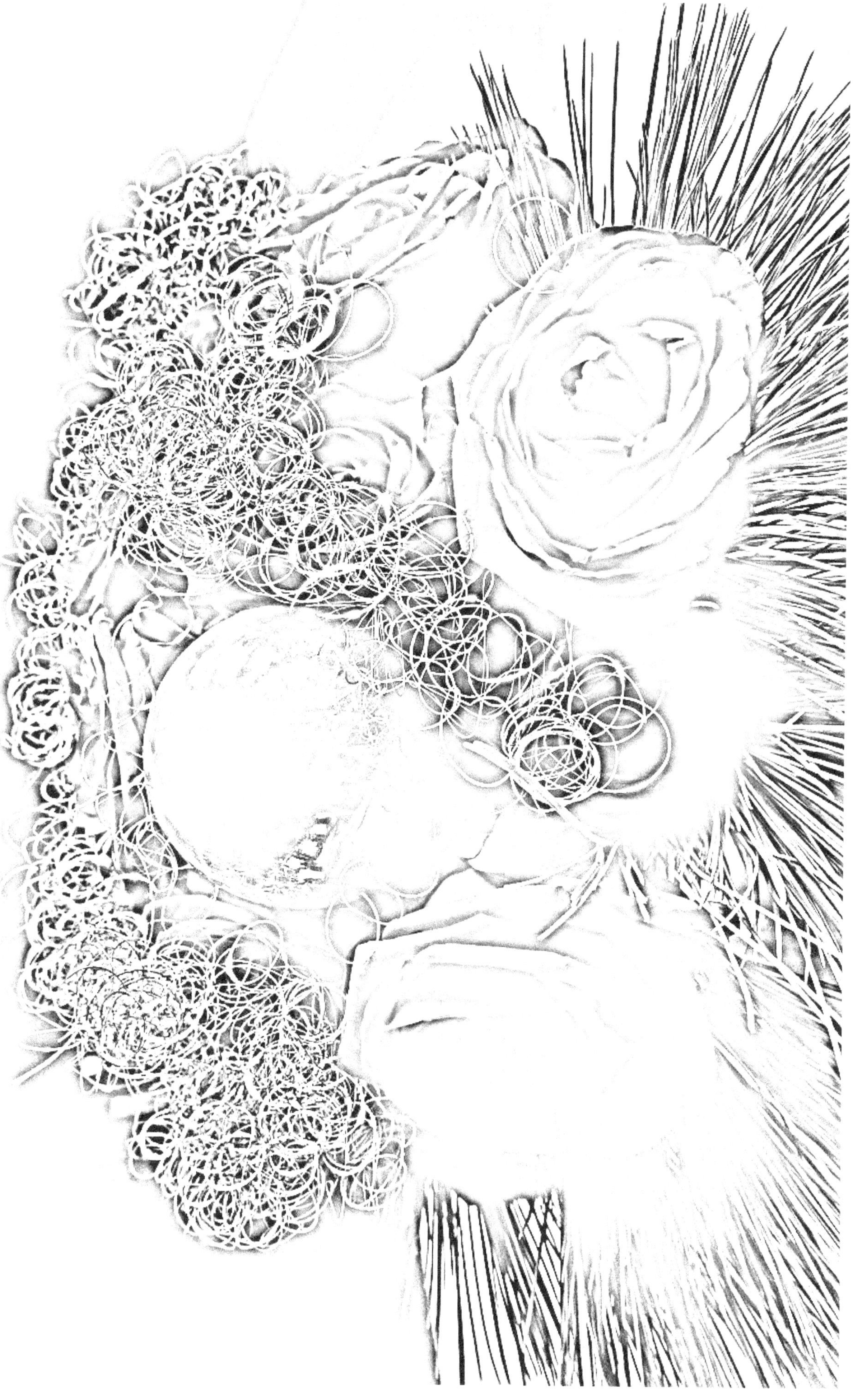

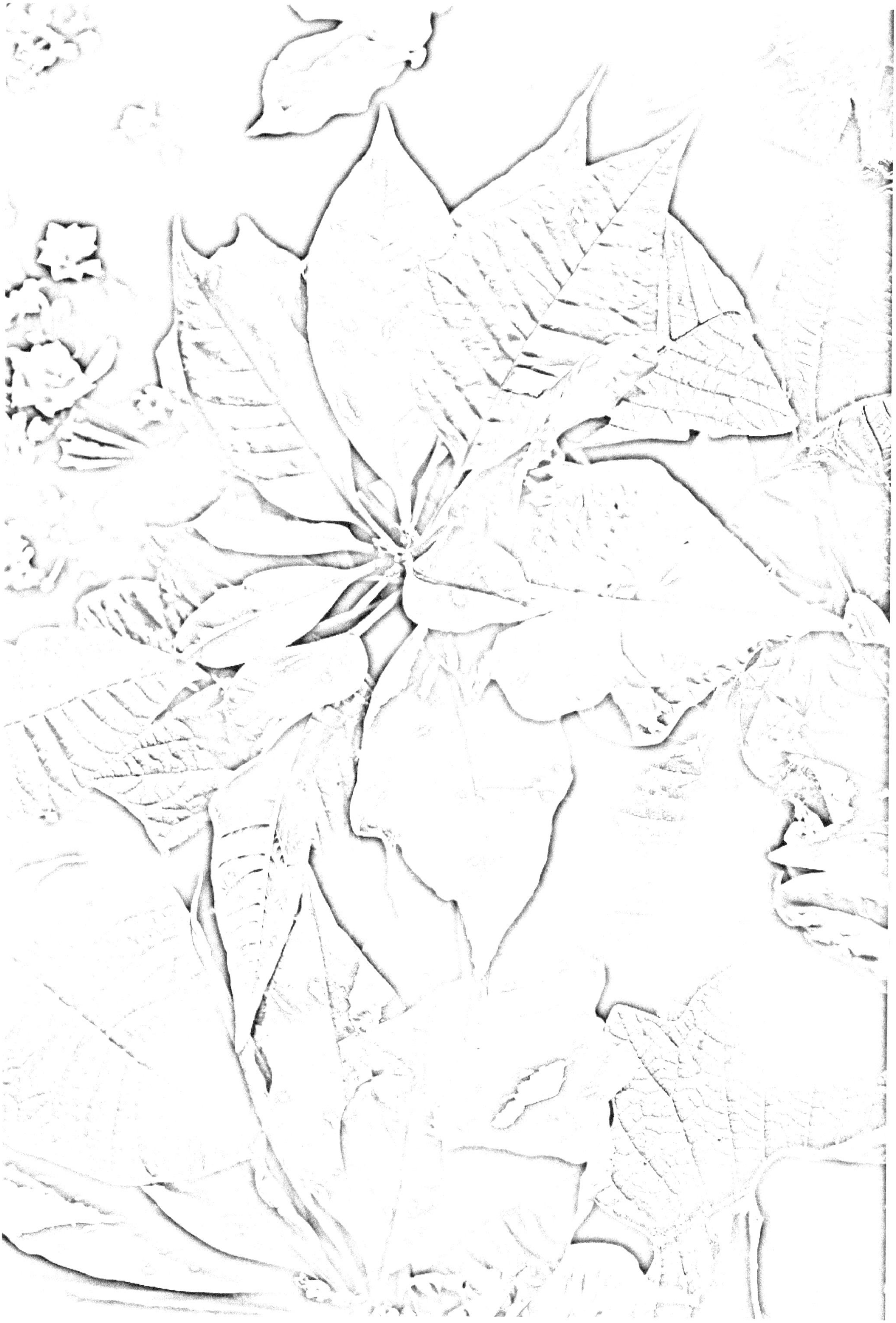

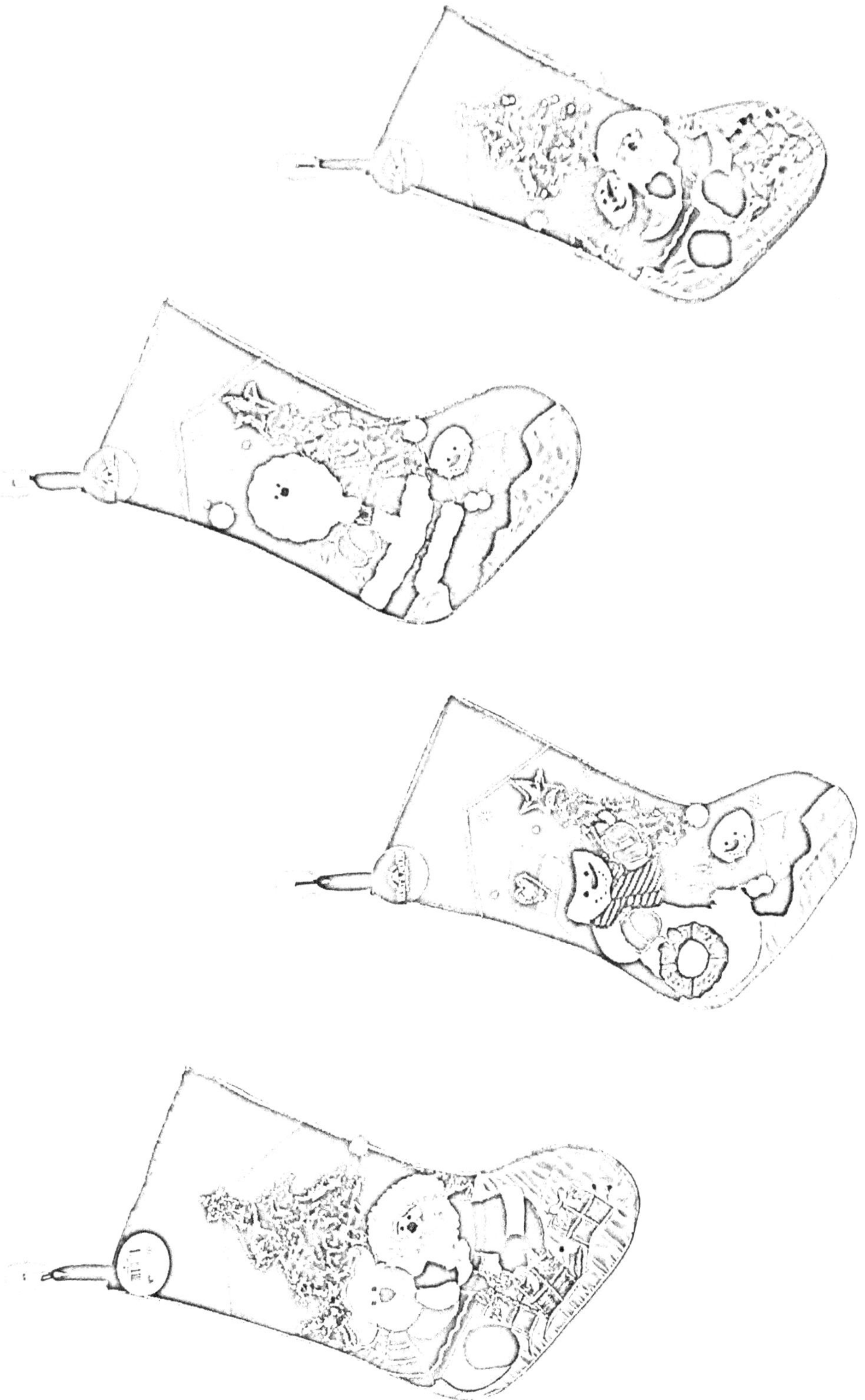

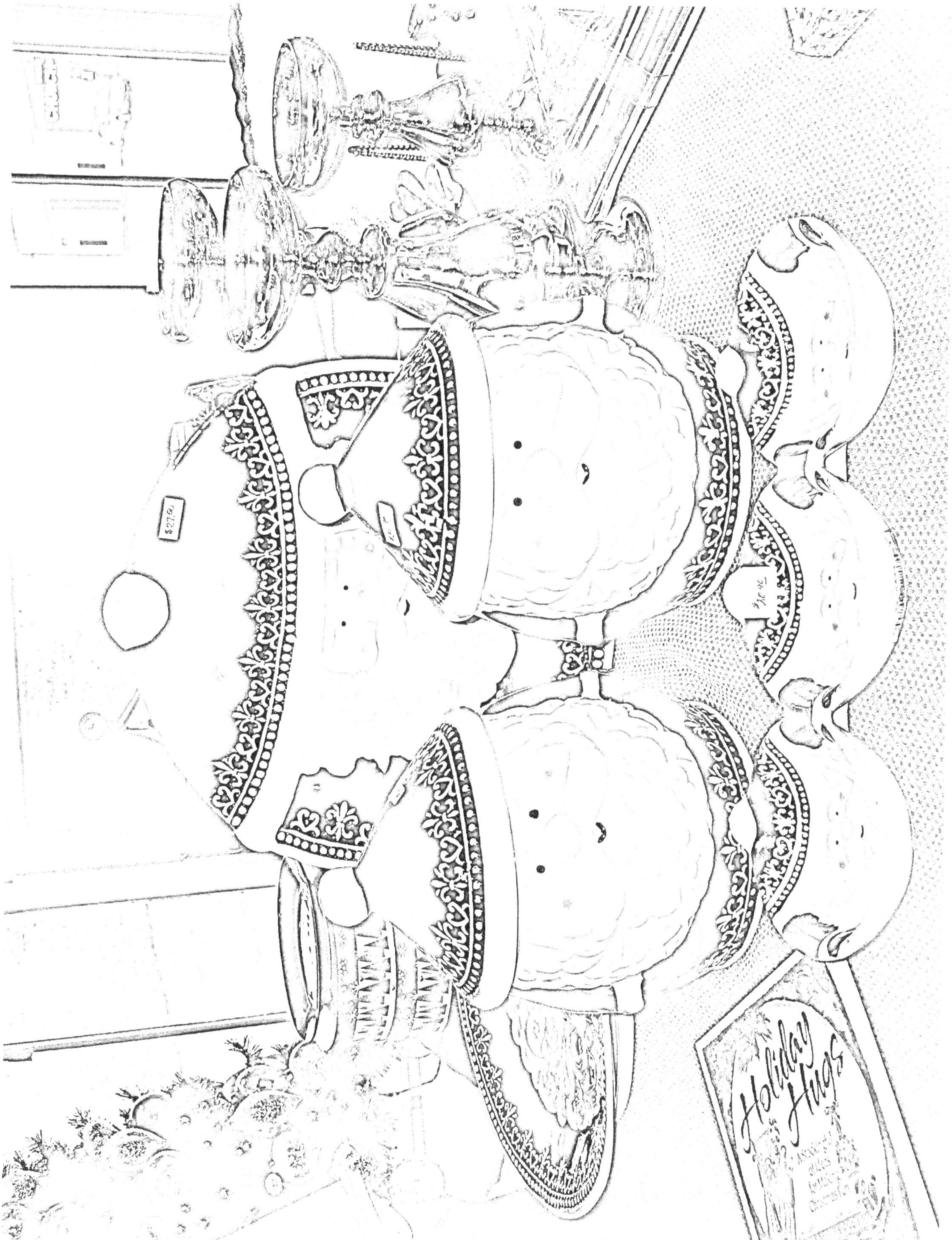
Holiday Hugs
$27.50

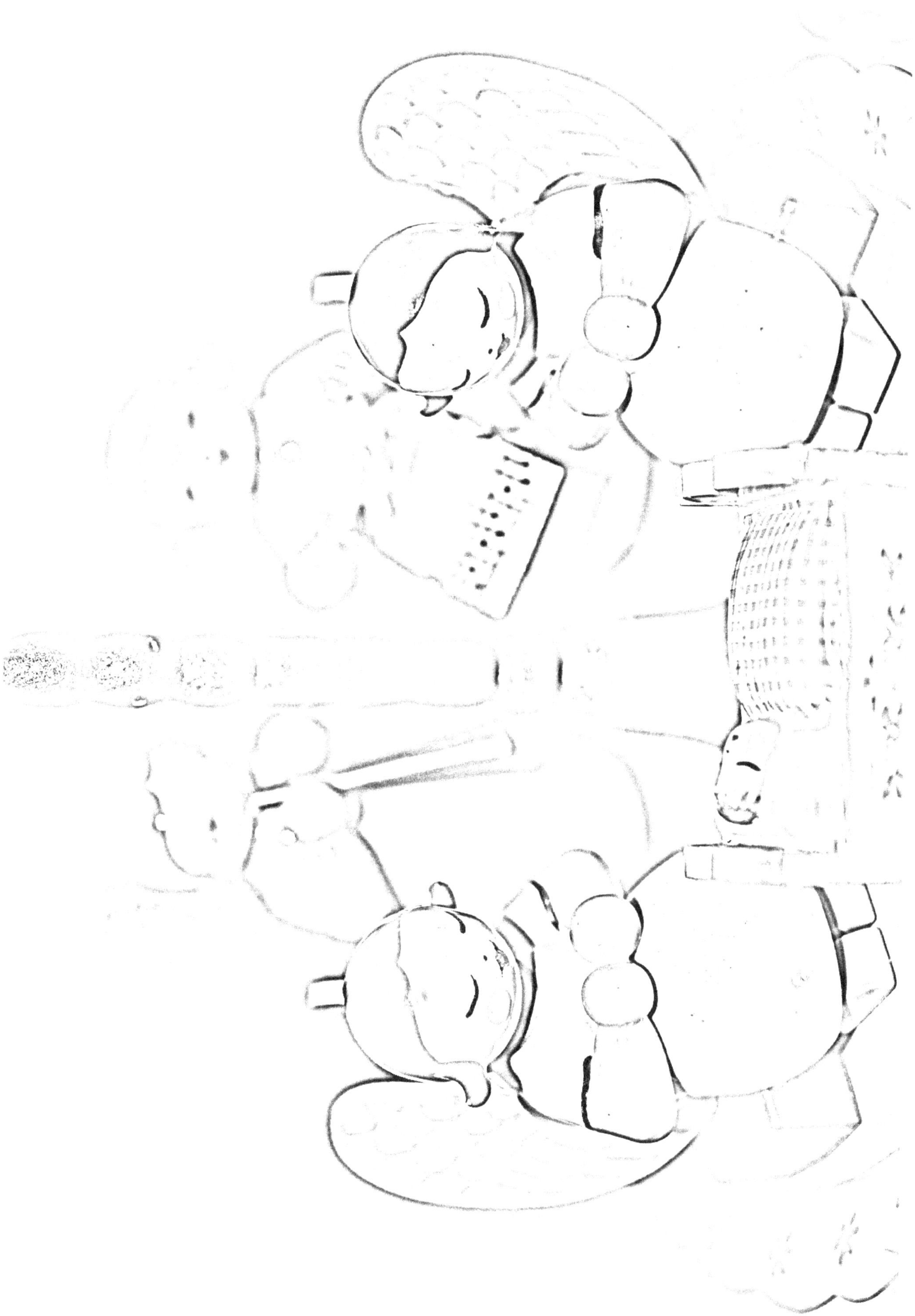

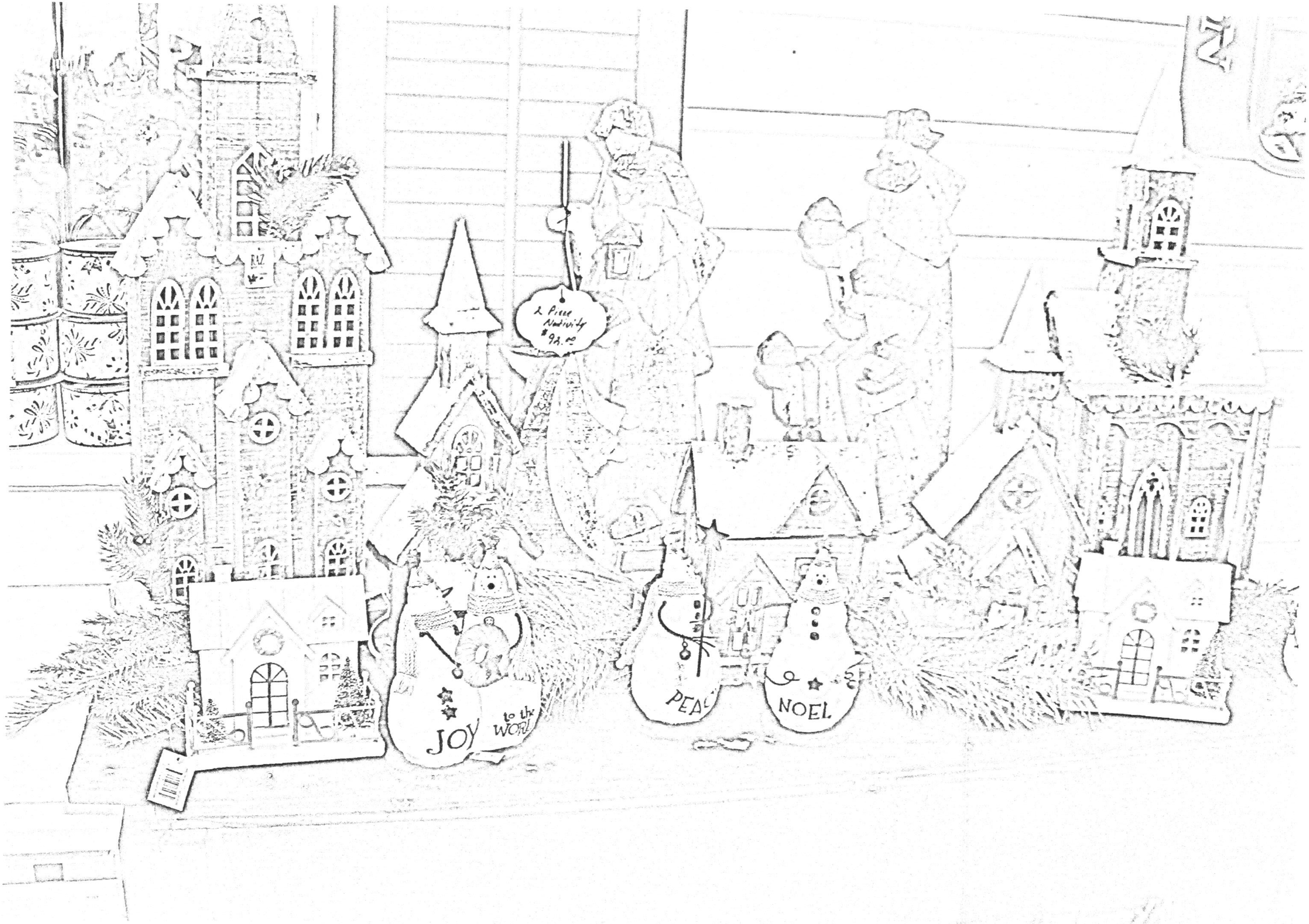
2 Piece Nativity
JOY
to the
NOEL

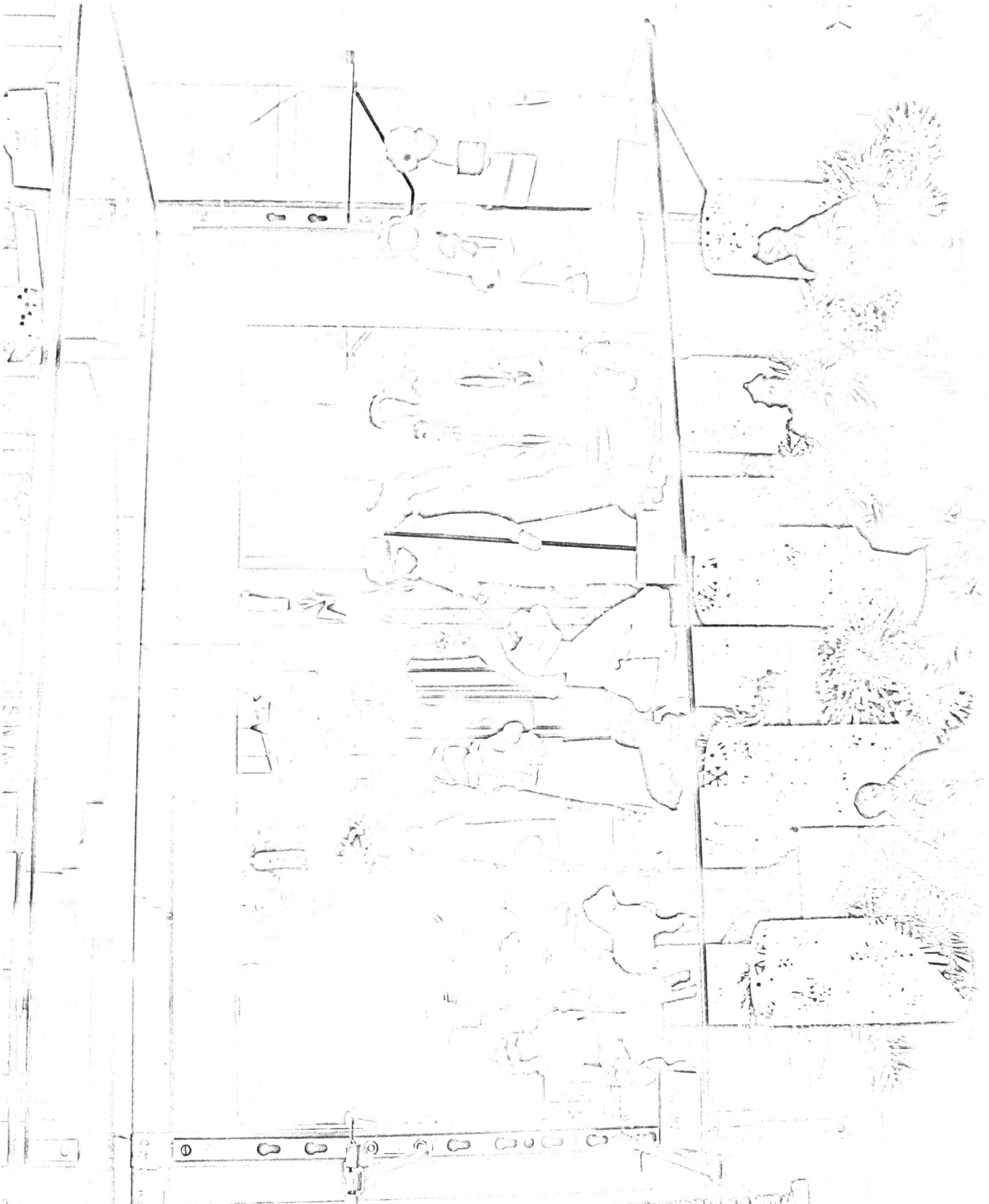

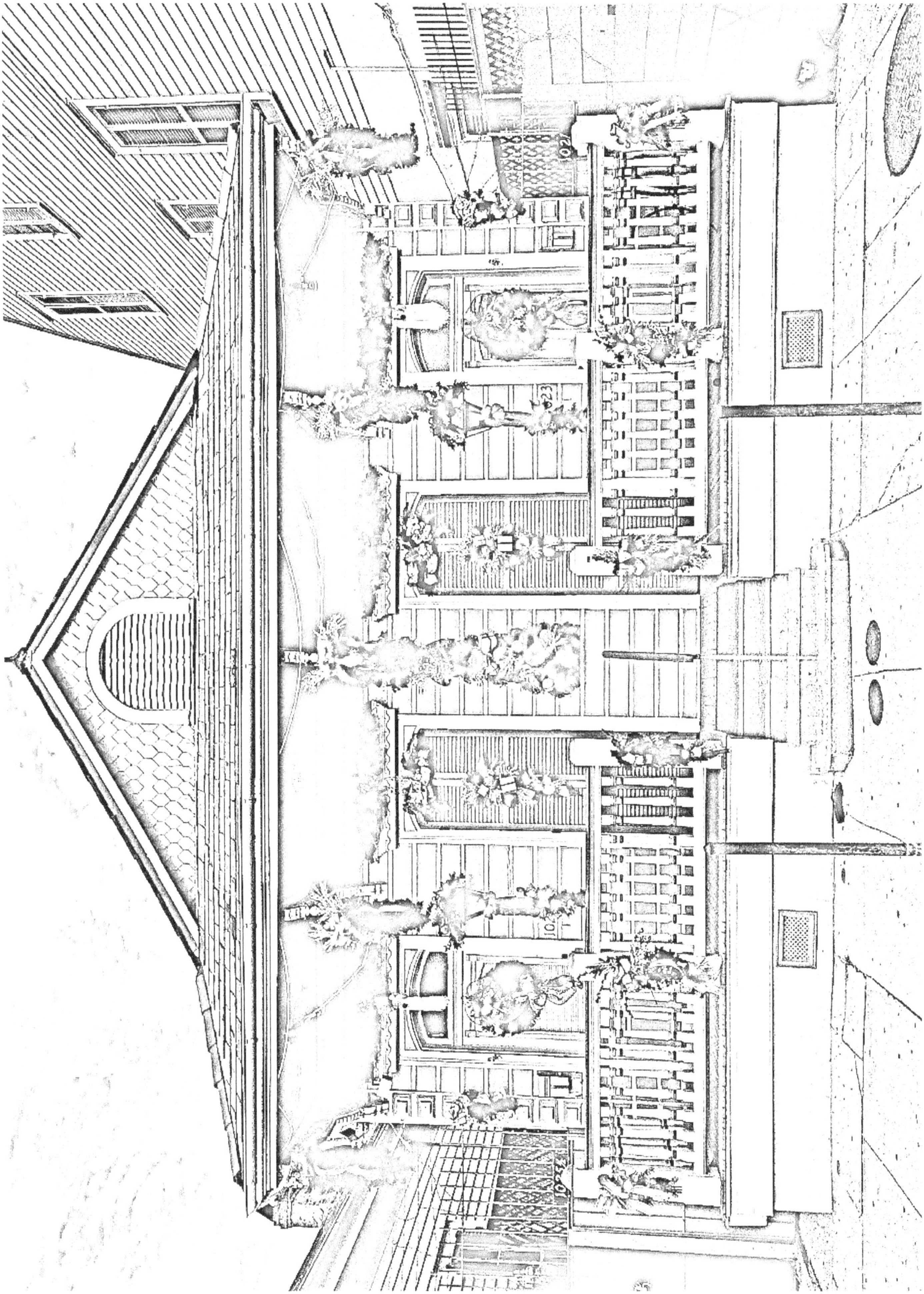

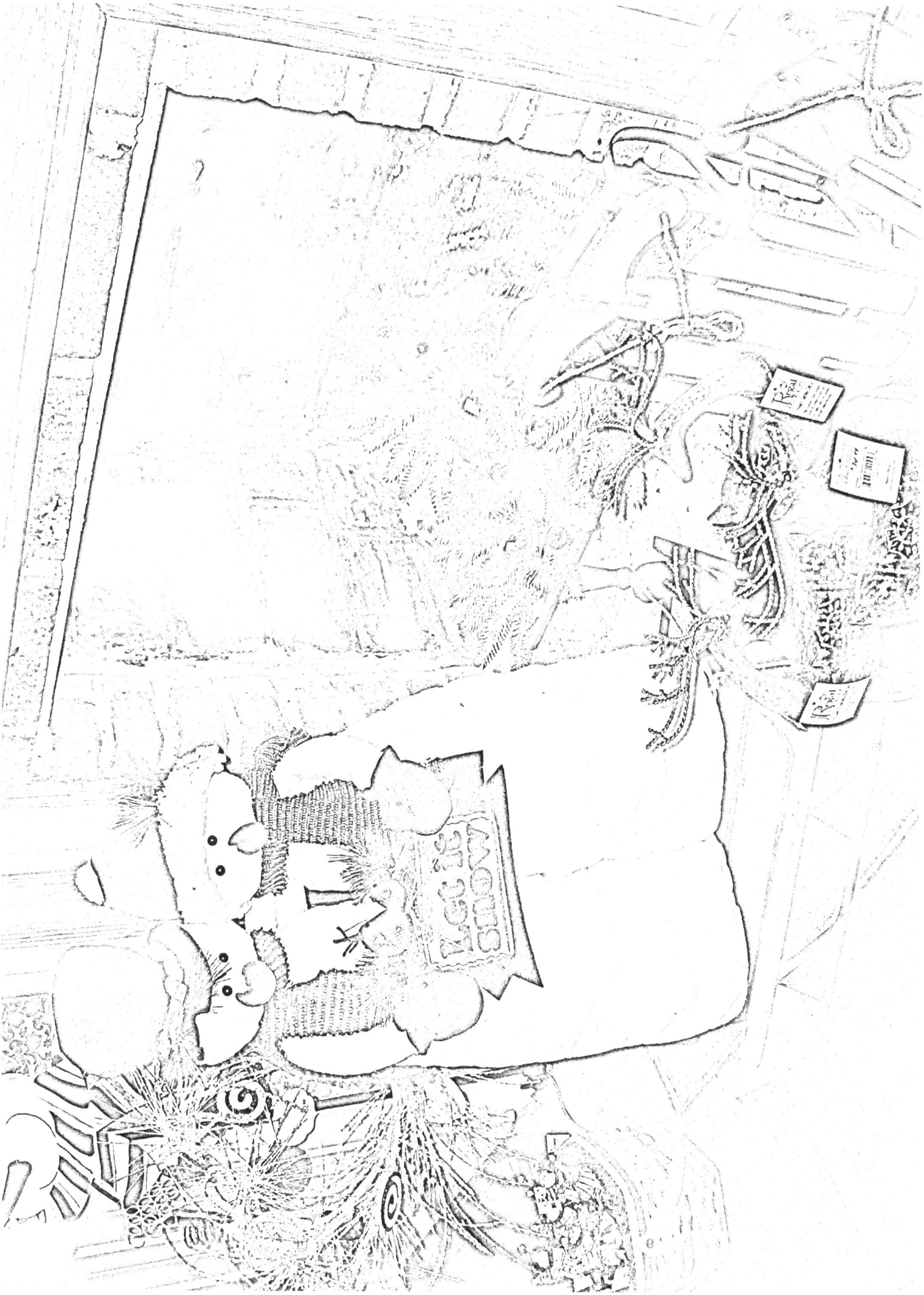
Let It Snow

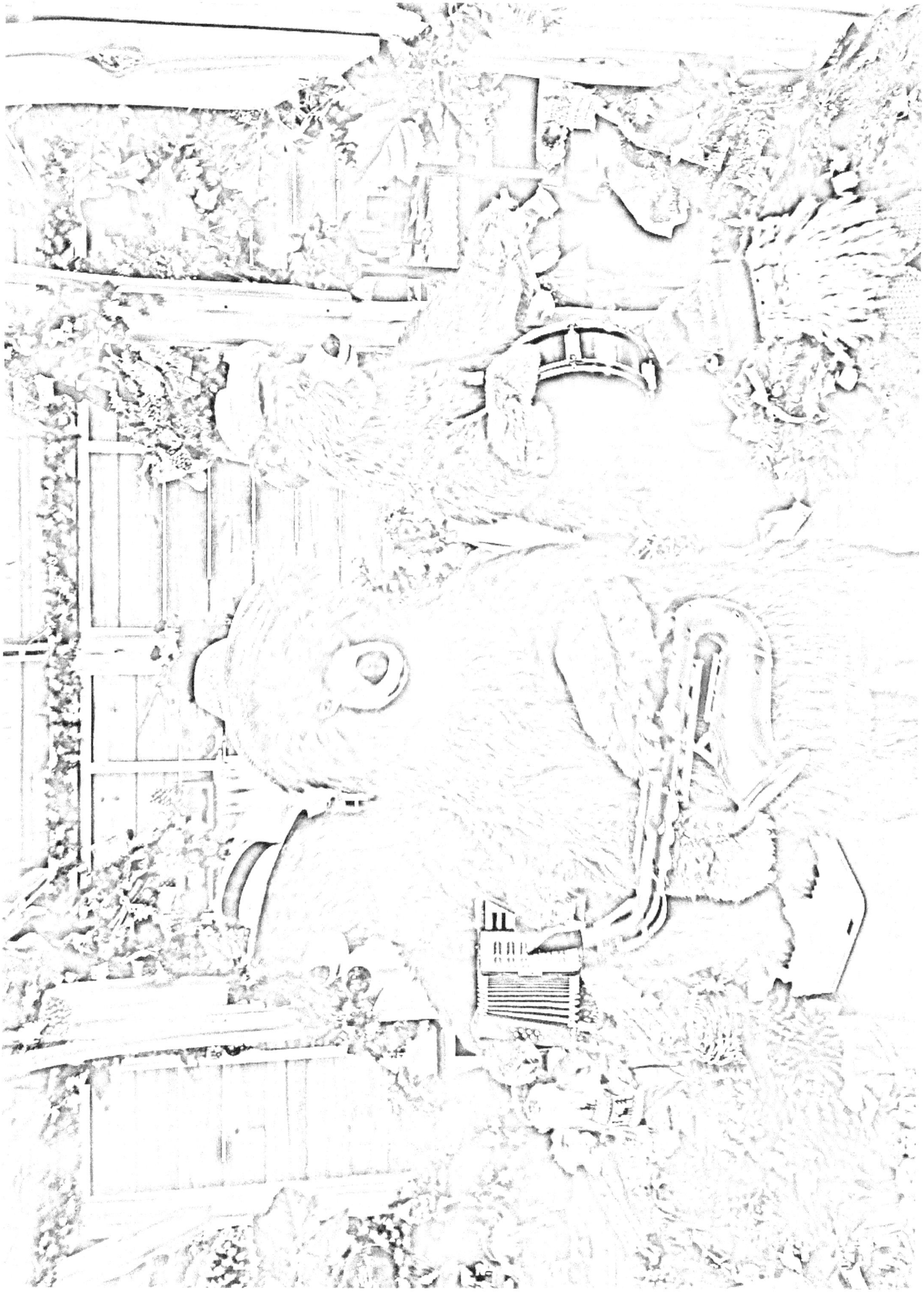

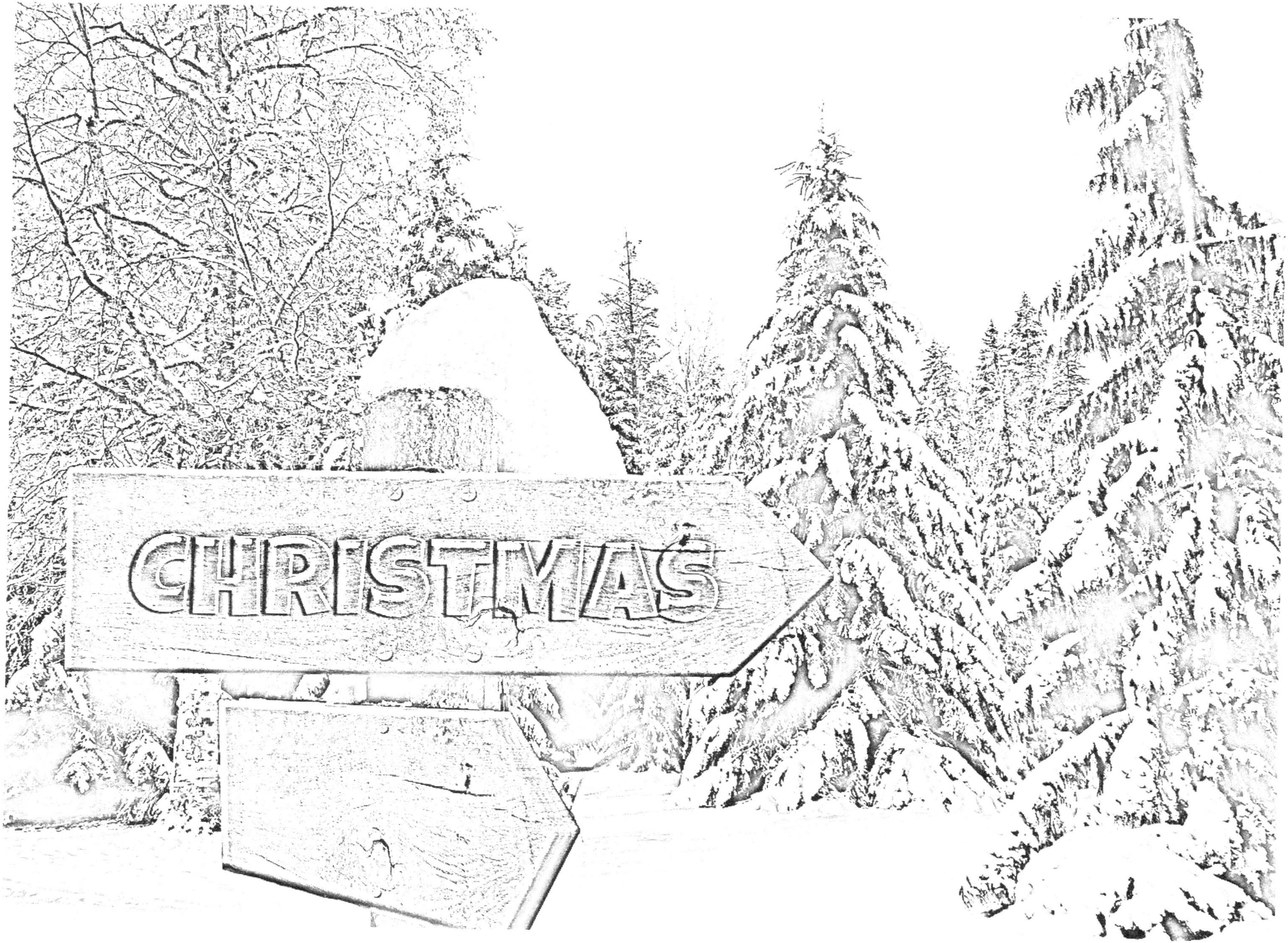
CHRISTMAS

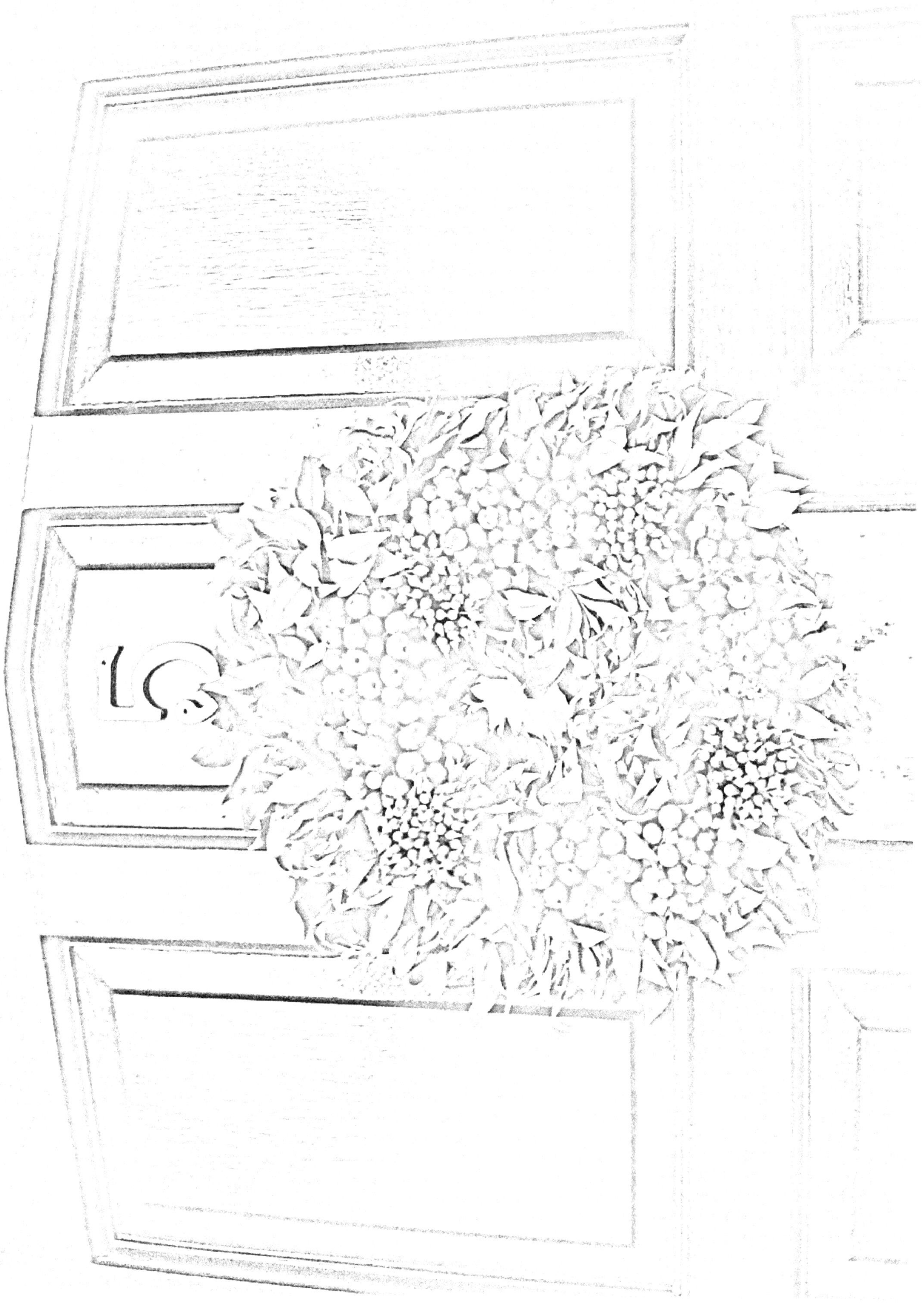
5

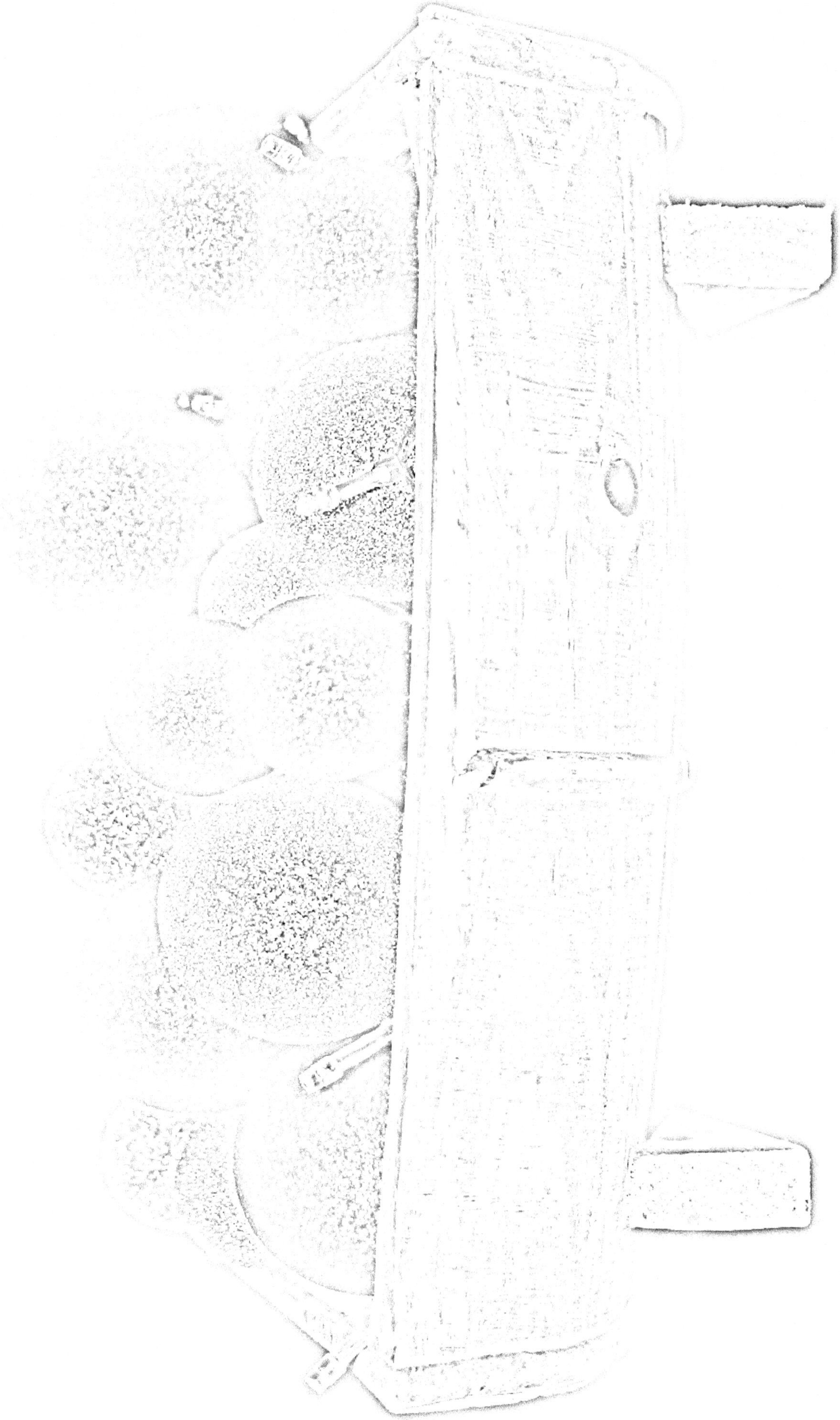

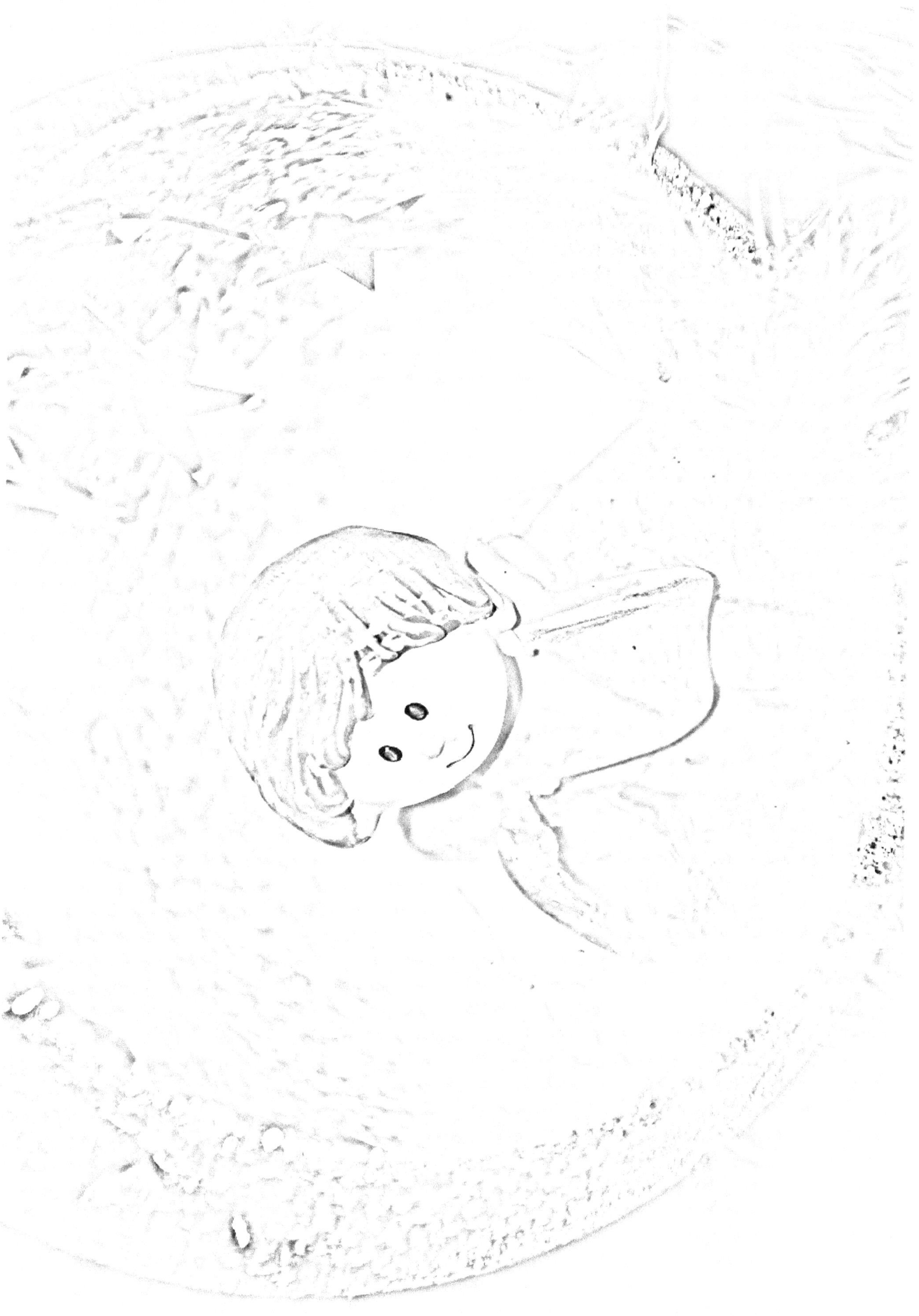

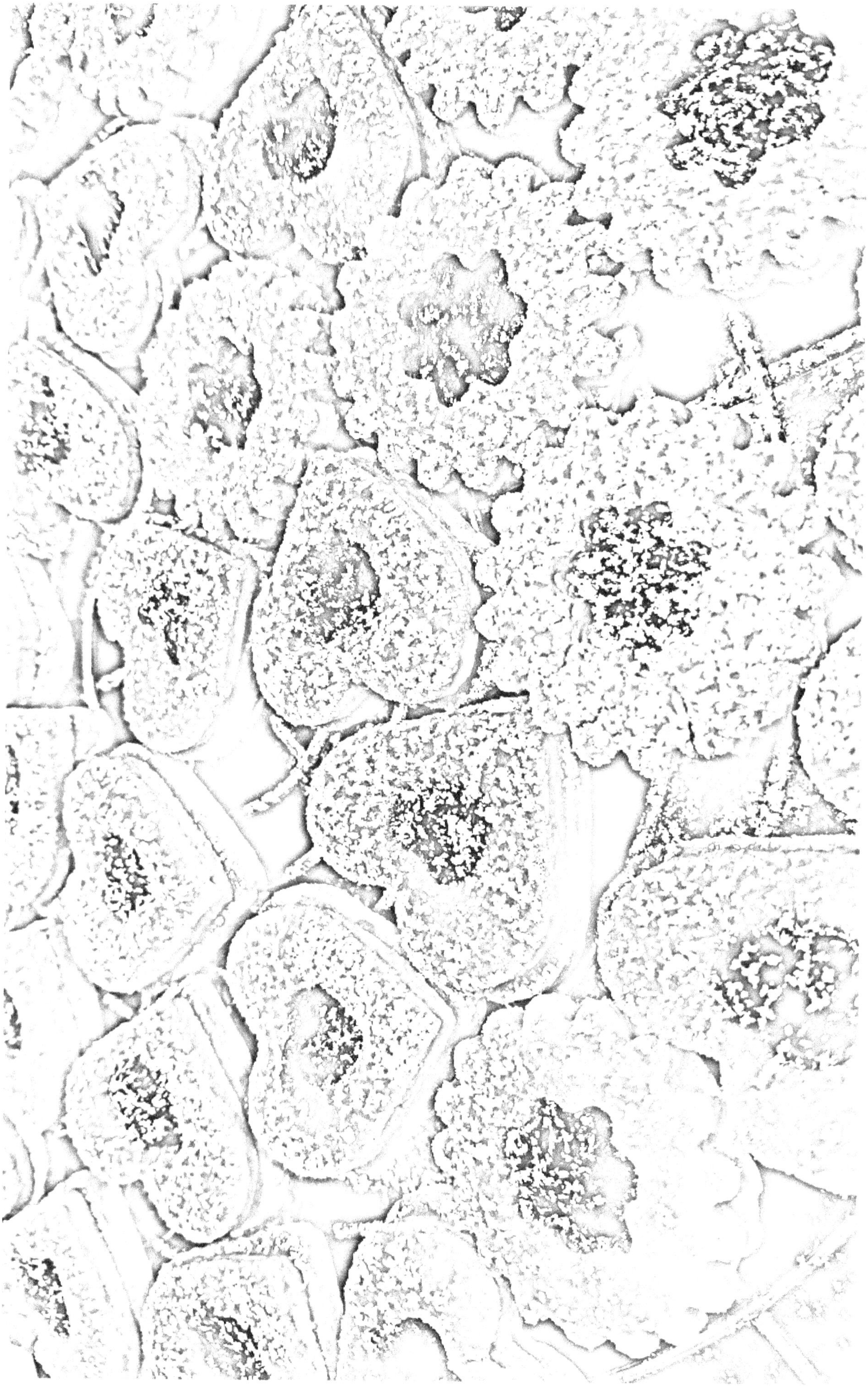

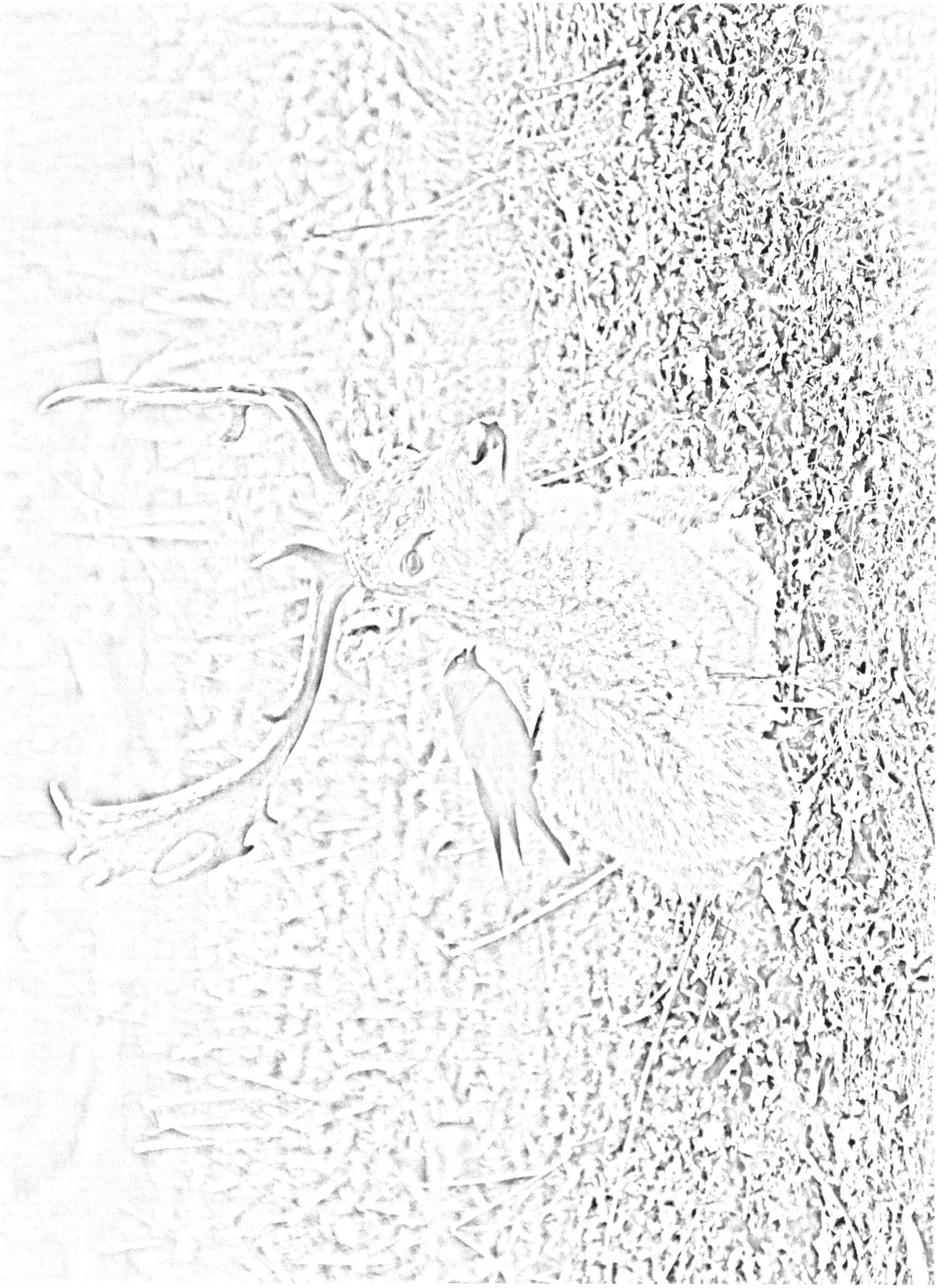

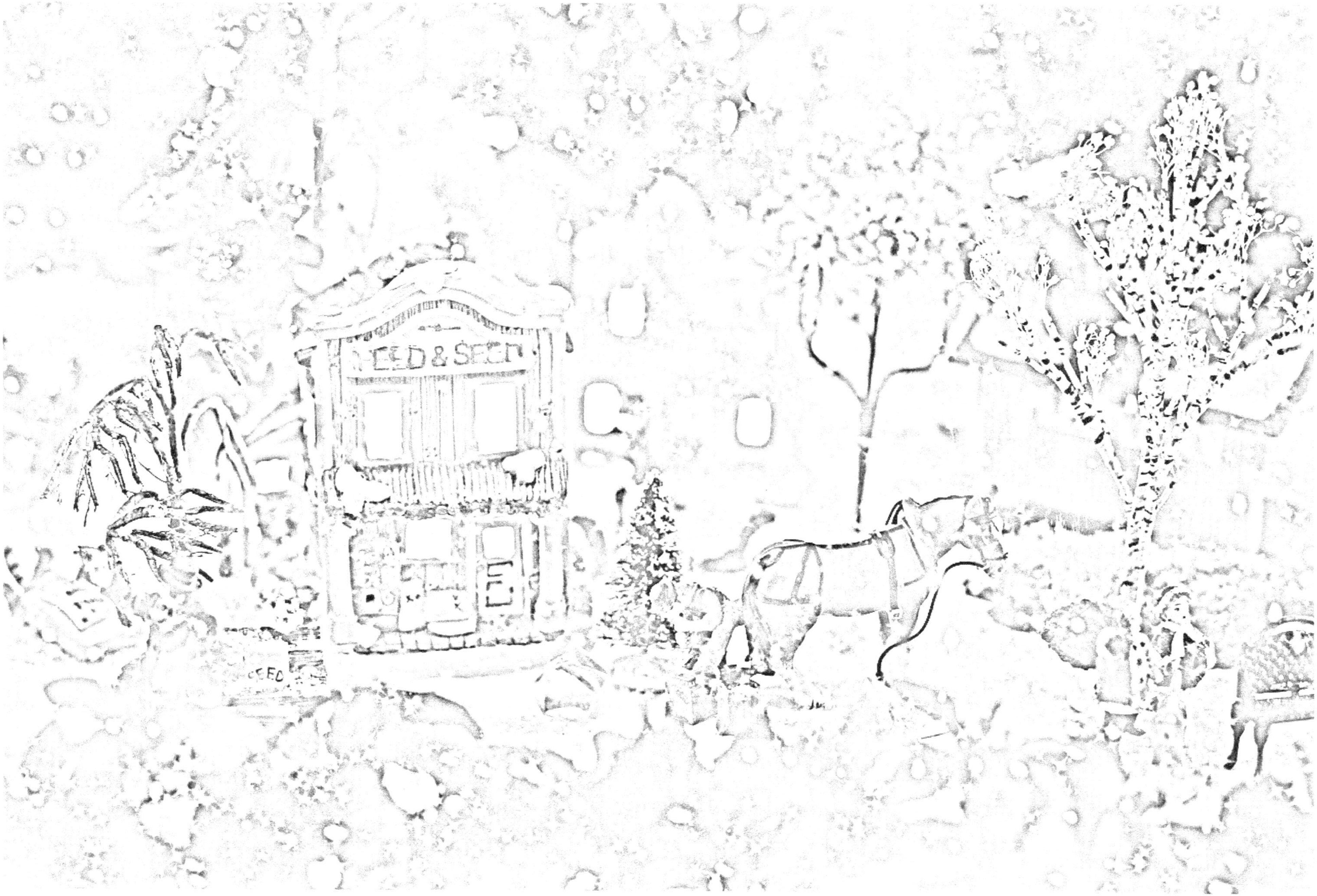
FEED & SEED

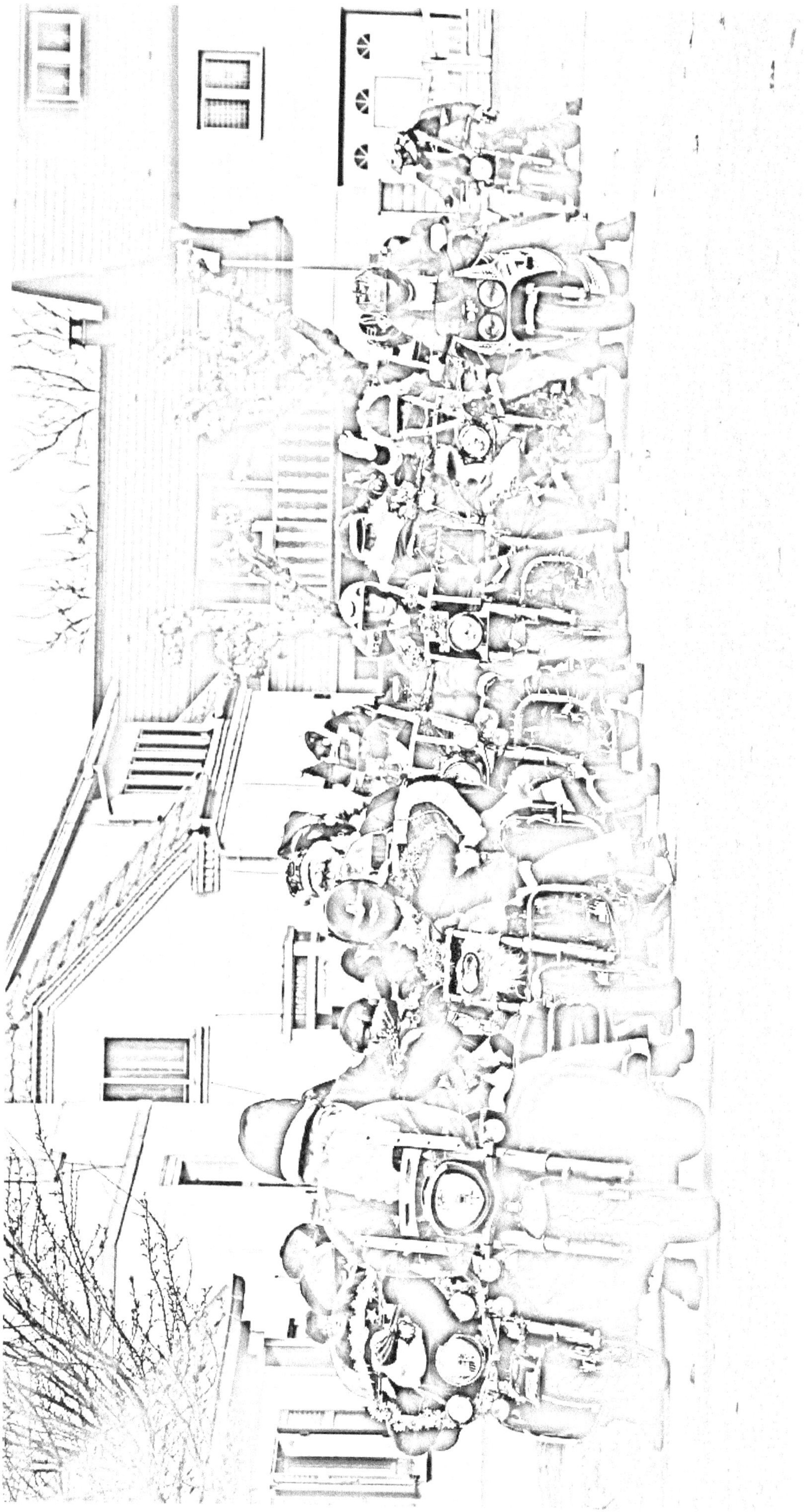

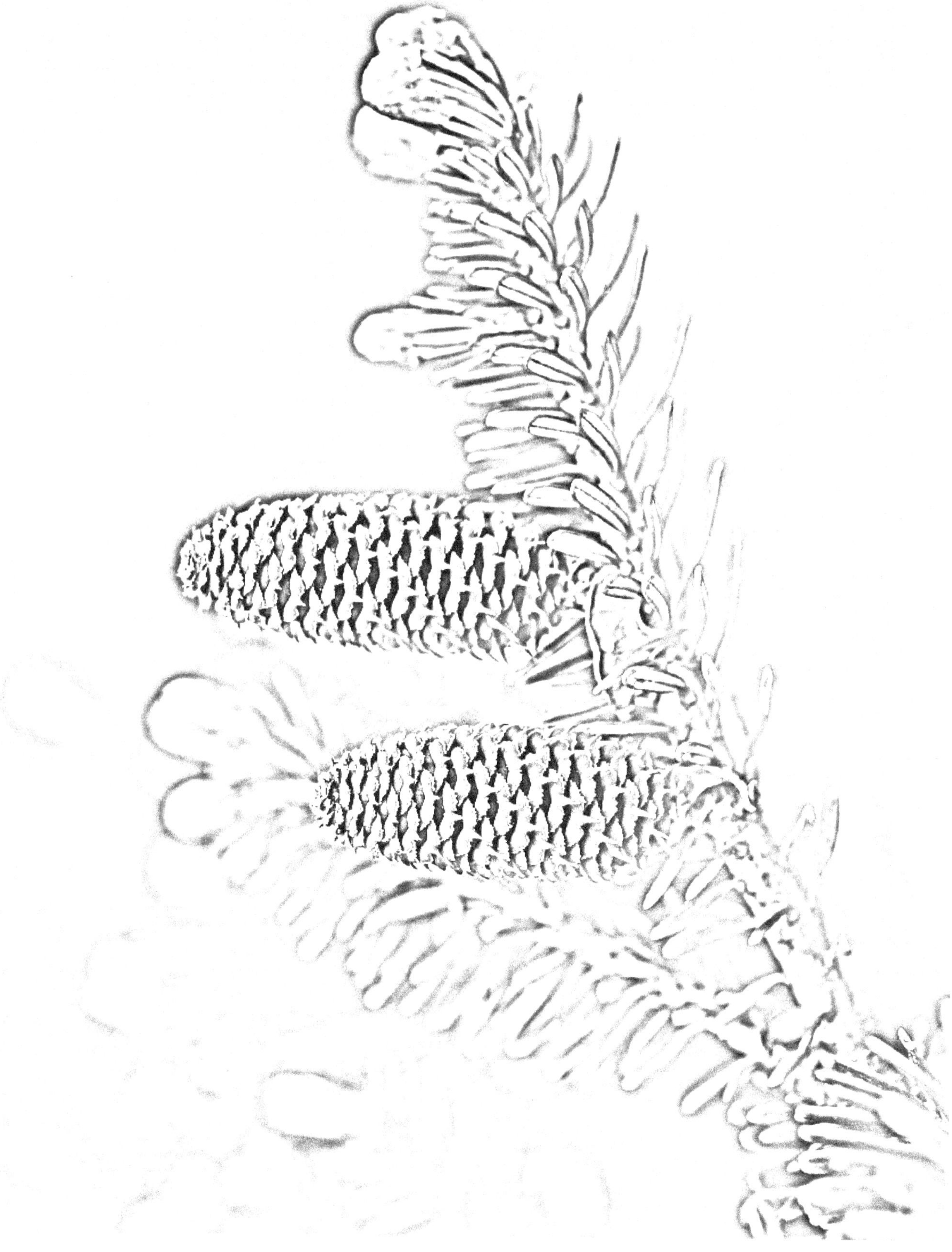

Merry Christmas!

We hope you enjoyed our book.

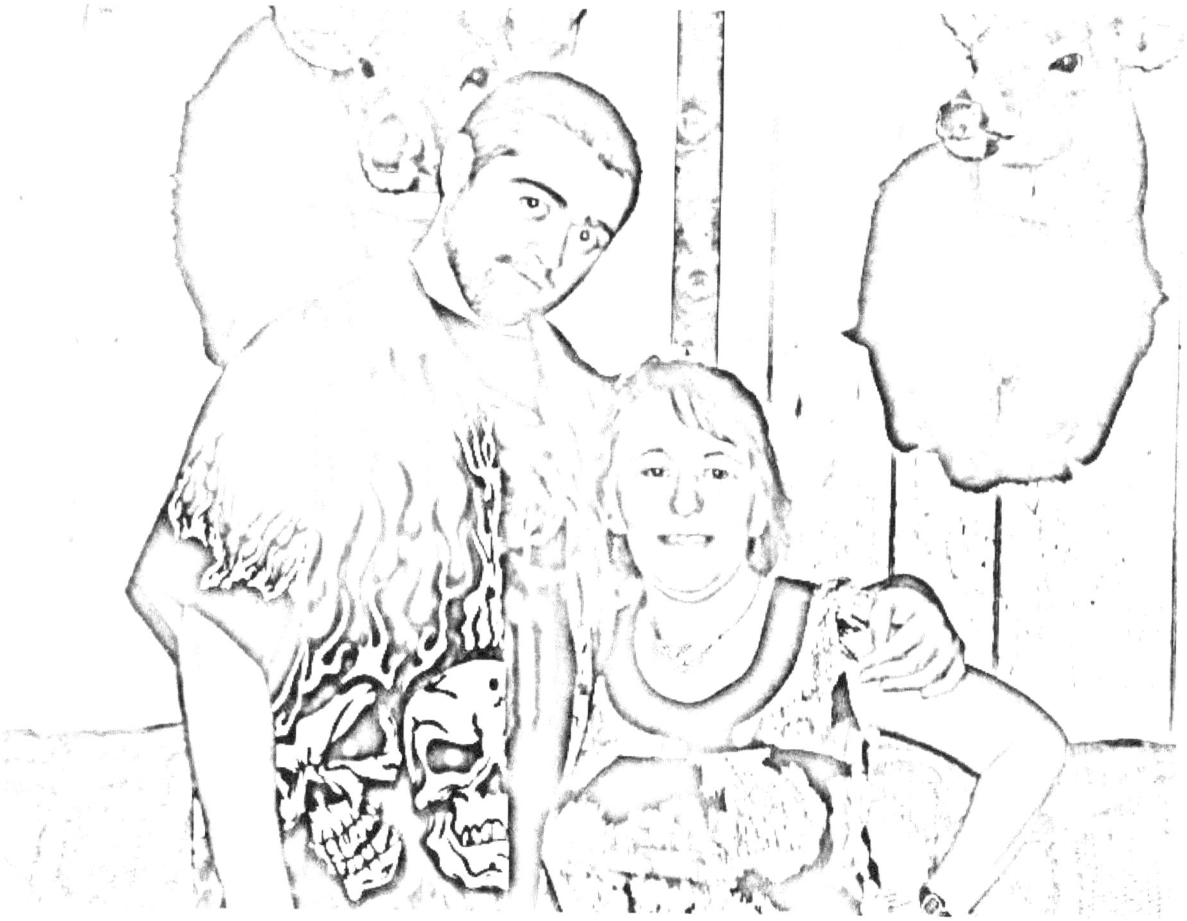

Watch for more coloring books by ARN Arts LLC.

http://arnarts.wixsite.com/books

www.ingramcontent.com/pod-product-compliance
Lightning Source LLC
Chambersburg PA
CBHW081124180526
45170CB00008B/2987